I0417103

# TABLE OF CONTENTS

DISCLAIMER AND TERMS OF USE AGREEMENT:

Introduction – Anti-Aging is What We Think About Often As We Age

Chapter 1 - Why We Age - Stress and immune response, stress and inflammation

Chapter 2 - Is Life Extension Possible?

Chapter 3 - Hydrogen Sulfide and Longevity - Life Extension and Hibernation

Chapter 4 - Calorie Restriction and Life Extension & Calorie Restriction and Life Expectancy - Cut Calories, Live Longer?

Chapter 5 - Can Suspended Animation Extend Life? - Suspended Animation...

Chapter 6 - Is Aging in Our Genes? Aging and Genetics - Genes and Successful Aging, DNA, genes & chromosomes, why enzymes are important

Chapter 7 - New Scientific Breakthroughs – Mitochondrial and Aging

Chapter 8 - Aging Glossary

I Have a Special Gift for My Readers

Meet the Author

**Anti Aging Techniques EXPOSED Vol 1**
Reversing the Aging Process
©Copyright 2013 Dr. Noah Pranksky

## DISCLAIMER AND TERMS OF USE AGREEMENT:

**(Please Read This Before Using This Book)**

This information is for educational and informational purposes only. The content is not intended to be a substitute for any professional advice, diagnosis, or treatment.

The authors and publisher of this book and the accompanying materials have used their best efforts in preparing this book.

The authors and publisher make no representation or warranties with respect to the accuracy, applicability, fitness, or completeness of the contents of this book. The information contained in this book is strictly for educational purposes. Therefore, if you wish to apply ideas contained in this book, you are taking full responsibility for your actions.

The authors and publisher disclaim any warranties (express or implied), merchantability, or fitness for any particular purpose. The author and publisher shall in no event be held liable to any party for any direct, indirect, punitive, special, incidental or other consequential damages arising directly or indirectly from any use of this material, which is provided "as is", and without warranties. As always, the advice of a competent legal, tax, accounting, medical or other professional should be sought where applicable.

The authors and publisher do not warrant the performance, effectiveness or applicability of any sites listed or linked to in this book. All links are for information purposes only and are not warranted for content, accuracy or any other implied or explicit purpose. No part of this may be copied, or changed in any format, or used in any way other than what is outlined within this course under any circumstances. Violators will be prosecuted.

This book is © Copyrighted by ePubWealth.com.

## Introduction – Anti-Aging is What We Think About Often As We Age

Aging! It is the stuff we all think about as we move up in years. This is not a new thought pattern; the thoughts of aging have been around since the dawn of man. Listen...

In Greek mythology, there is a story about a mortal youth named Tithonus. Aurora, the goddess of dawn, fell in love with the boy and when Zeus, the king of the gods, promised to grant Aurora any gift she chose for her lover, she asked that Tithonus might live forever. But, in her haste, she forgot to ask for eternal youth, so when Zeus granted her request, Tithonus was doomed to an eternity of perpetual aging as a bent and grouchy old man... forever.

I must confess something to you; Greek mythology has always fascinated me. Without knowing it, the Greeks served up some pretty good stuff through their feeble fantasies and stories. They just didn't know it! The story of Tithonus is one such example.

To the Greeks, they could only understand the meaning of eternal life through mortal eyes. To them, eternal life had stages of aging similar to mortal life. In our story, perpetual youth had to be specifically requested in their plea to their god Zeus. In other words, they combined worldly ideals with spiritual concepts.

**The Greeks had it almost right, but it is still wrong.**

And what they had was counterfeit to the truth. The only thing that decides counterfeits are things that are valuable in everyone's eyes. No one on the planet counterfeits Monopoly money, but they do counterfeit US currency. So, only the things that are valuable are worth counterfeiting, right? Truth is always worth counterfeiting because it is valuable.

**I guess one has to be quite careful with what one asks for.**


Your treasure is exactly where your heart is, and your heart is your subconscious mind. These treasures are belief systems and evoke the corresponding behavior and conduct.

Aurora got exactly what she asked for, and Tithonus suffered for her actions. So let's get it right and make sure you get it right.

## Chapter 1 - Why We Age - Stress and immune response, stress and inflammation

The study of aging is called "gerontology" and is a relatively new science that has made incredible progress over the last 30 years. In an attempt to answer questions on aging, scientists are asking questions like "is aging natural and programmed into the body" or "is aging the result of damage which is accumulated over time?"

Theories of Aging propose that aging is a complex interaction of genetics, chemistry, physiology and behavior. We will be looking at several theories as we move through this book

1. The human body is designed to age and there is a certain timeline that our bodies follow.
2. Aging is caused by gene switching. Pre-determined genes that turn on and off over time.
3. Changes in amounts and structure of hormones control aging.
4. The immune system is declines over time for a variety of reasons, leaving people more susceptible to diseases.
5. Aging is caused by environmental damage to our body's systems.
6. Cells and tissues simply wear out.
7. The faster an organism uses oxygen, the shorter it lives.
8. Cross-linked proteins accumulate and slow down body processes.
9. Free radicals cause damage to cells that eventually impairs function.
10. Genetic mutations cause cells to malfunction.

## Genetics and Aging

Do genetics play a major role in aging? Researchers have found that by adjust the genes in certain mice, yeast cells and other organisms; they can almost double the lifespan of these creatures. The meaning of these experiments is at best ambiguous, but researchers are proposing that genetics accounts for up to 35 percent of the aging equation

1. There are specific genes which help a person live longer.
2. Cell Senescence - The process by which cells deteriorate over time.

3. Telomeres - Structures on the end of DNA that eventually are depleted, resulting in cells ceasing to replicate.
4. Stem Cells - These cells can become any type of cell in the body and hold promise to repair damage caused by aging.

**Biochemistry**

Your body is continually undergoing complex biochemical reactions regardless of what genes you have inherited. These reactions can cause damage and the result is that the body ages. By studying these complex reactions, researchers understand how the body changes as it ages. Important concepts in the biochemistry of aging include:

1. Free Radicals: Unstable oxygen molecules can damage cells.
2. Protein Cross-Linking: Excess sugars in the blood stream can cause protein molecules to literally stick together.
3. DNA Repair: the systems in the body to repair DNA seem to become less effective in older people.
4. Heat Shock Proteins: Proteins help cells survive stress and there are fewer of these proteins in older people.
5. Hormones: As we age, body's hormones change causing changes in organ systems and other functions.

**Body Systems**

As we age, our body's organs and other systems make changes; some are obvious and visible while others occur within the body itself. These changes can change our immune system's ability to fend off various diseases. Researchers haven't even begun to understand how, as we age, the processes that cause changes in our body systems.

1. As we age, the heart muscle thickens as a response to the thickening of the arteries. This thicker heart has a lower maximum pumping rate.
2. In older people, T-cells take longer to replenish and their ability to function declines.
3. As we age, arteries usually to stiffen making it more difficult for the heart to pump blood through them.
4. Lung capacity may decrease as much as 40 percent between ages 20 and 70.
5. Some of the connections between neurons seem to be reduced or less efficient as the brain ages.
6. With age, the kidneys become less efficient at cleaning waste from the body.
7. Bladder capacity declines with age and tissues may atrophy, causing incontinence.
8. Up and until middle age, body fat increases and then weight typically begins to decrease. Body fat also settles deeper into the body as we age.
9. By age 70, muscle tone declines about 22 percent. Exercise can slow this decline.
10. Bones begin to lose density beginning at the age of 35. Walking, running and resistance training can slow this process.

11. Difficulty seeing close detail may begin in the 40s.
12. The ability to hear high frequencies declines with age.

## Behavioral Factors

Behavioral modification may change the way we age. By eating proper foods loaded with antioxidants, damage can be minimized caused by free radicals. Proper and continuous exercising, you can limit bone and muscle loss. Low cholesterol can slow the hardening of your arteries and protect your heart. Mental fitness is determined by how often you exercise your brain too. Dietary factors have shown to extend life. Rats and mice on a calorie restricted diet (30 percent fewer daily calories) live up to 40 percent longer. Positive mental thinking has also been shown to extend life in people by up to 7.5 years.

## Aging is Programmed

The question arises; is aging an essential and innate part of the biology? Is aging is programmed into our body systems? Three main body systems are affected by aging - endocrine (hormonal) system, the immune system and our genes. All three of these systems are altered as we age and these changes cause the symptoms and signs of aging.

## The Body is NOT a Machine

The human body is often compared to a machine but it is not a machine. A machine has only the parts it was built with but the human body is continually repairing and replacing cells. No machine can repair itself. About every seven years, almost 90 percent of the cells in our bodies are renewed. Yes, the human body is the most amazing, open, and dynamic system ever created but to understand aging, we have to think about living systems.

## Aging Is About Evolution, Not Biology

The question most often asked is this: "should the human body "wear out?" After all, as stated above, the human body can repair and renew itself. Time may be one factor in the aging of the body but there must be other factors at play to cause the inevitable effects of aging. This question leads to the programmed theory of aging that believes aging and death are necessary parts of evolution but not of biology. Species of all types require a genetic capacity for aging and death; otherwise it would not be forced to replicate to survive. Species would just keep on living until a climate or other change wiped them all out. If biological individuals live forever, there would be no evolution.

## Programmed Aging

Aging is inherent in the organism and not the result of environmental factors or sickness; hence, aging and death, are not a direct result of wear and tear or exposure, but is a programmed response that is a natural and necessary part of genetics. In short, we are programmed to age and die. The evidence demonstrates that there is not a great deal of variation in lifespan within species. Elephants die around 70, spider monkeys die around 25, and people die around 80. Changes in diet and lifestyle can be made based on nutrition and medical care -- but overall lifespan within species is fairly constant. In other words, good nutrition and healthy habits causes a high

11

quality of life but does not determine quantity of life. If aging were due to "wear and tear" there would be more variation in lifespan within each species.

## Hormones Make Us Old

The most important aspects of aging are the changes brought about in the body by the endocrine system. The endocrine system controls the hormones that regulate many body processes. These systems become less efficient as we age leading to changes in our bodies such as menopause. To demonstrate this, researchers removed the pituitary gland of mice. This gland controls much of the endocrine system. Then, the mice were given all of the hormones that are currently known to substitute for the absence of the pituitary gland. The mice without a pituitary gland lived longer than normal mice. It is obvious that the pituitary must also excrete another, unknown, hormone that negatively impacts aging. Hormonal changes are an important part of aging but it is unlikely that hormone substitution in humans will increase lifespan and can even be dangerous. Some anti-aging doctors will prescribe human growth hormone (HGH), but subsequent studies show this to be unwise in many ways. Synthetic HGH is used to treat dwarfism and not enough research has been conducted to determine if it is safe to use as an anti-aging agent. It is interesting to note that the human body produces natural HGH by the pituitary gland and that natural stimulation of this process is sleep and strenuous exercise.

## The Immune System is to Blame

The immune system theory of aging is that the rate of aging is largely controlled by the immune system. As we age, the numbers of critical cells in the immune system decrease and become less functional. Starting before age 20, the thymus (which produced certain immune cells) begins to shrink.

## How These Changes Affect the Body:

The immune system is important in keeping our bodies healthy. Not only does it protect us against viruses and bacteria, it also helps to identify and remove cancer cells and toxins. As we age, the potential for these elements to cause damage in our bodies increases.

## We Just Wear Out

The wear and tear of aging results by damage done to cells and body systems over time. These systems simply "wear out" due to use and in many cases overuse such as high carb and sugar diets wearing out the pancreas to a point where it can no longer function correctly. Damage to body systems is the result of many factors. Exposure to radiation, toxins and ultraviolet light can damage our genes. It has now been proven that over-exposure to microwave ovens is harmful. Our bodies own functioning can also cause damage. When the body metabolizes oxygen, free radicals are produced that can cause damage to cells and tissues. Yes, the capacity of the body to repair damage is designed into our physiology but not all damage can be fully repaired. Mistakes in repairing the body may accumulate over time. A decrease may actually be is the result and not the cause of aging.

## Live Fast, Die Young

Perhaps one of the oldest thoughts of aging is the rate of living theory. It is thought that people as well as other creatures have a finite number of breaths, heartbeats or other measures. In ancient times, people believed that the human body deteriorates in direct proportion to its use. Today, scientists recognize that the number of heartbeats does not predict lifespan and now believe that the speed at which an organism processes oxygen is a better and more accurate measurement. There is some evidence that creatures with faster oxygen metabolisms die younger. Tiny mammals with rapid heartbeats metabolize oxygen quickly and have short life spans. Tortoises, on the other hand, metabolize oxygen very slowly and have long life spans. Scientists genetically engineered mice with a defect in the hypothalamus part of the brain to cause the mice to overexert. Because the hypothalamus in mice is near the temperature control center, the mice's brain thought the body was overheating and lowered the core temperature.

The results show that a drop of .6 degrees Celsius extended the life of the mice by 12 to 20 percent. The lower temperature may slow the rate of oxygen metabolism. The problem is that the lower temperature may also change a number of other systems and processes in the body. We don't know why the mice lived longer, only that they did. Oxygen metabolism, heartbeat or the number of breaths determine an individual's lifespan is poor evidence to support this theory. The theory can only partially explain the differences in lifespan among species. It cannot explain the most important factor: what determines lifespan within species. For example, if a person lives 100 years, they have taken far more breaths, metabolized more oxygen and had more heartbeats than someone who only lives until 80.

What we want to know, from a longevity perspective, is what determines which individuals within a species live the longest. There really is no data that slowing the metabolism extends human life. In fact, a slower metabolism would put someone at risk for obesity and other nutritional-related illnesses. Your best bet is still a healthy lifestyle with plenty of exercise, a diet with lots of plants, and a positive, relaxed attitude.

## Sugar Makes You Old

Whenever you heat onions or toast bread, the sugar molecules bond to protein molecules. This bonding is called carmalization. When this happens, a series of reactions occur (called glycation) that result in protein molecules bonding to each other. The process is slow and complicated, but over time more and more protein molecules are cross-linked. These cross-linked molecules don't function properly. When enough cross-linked molecules accumulate in a specific tissue (such as cartilage, lungs, arteries and tendons), there can be a change in function. With cross-linking, things become stiffer and when tissues stiffen, they do not function as efficiently. Many of the symptoms of aging have to do with the stiffening of tissues. Cataracts, for example, are a stiffening of your eyes' lenses. Cross-linking cannot be stopped but you can slow it down. Scientists now believe that when the concentration of sugar in the blood is high, more cross-linking occurs. Everyone could benefit from keeping their blood sugar from spiking. Foods with a high glycemic index, such as sugary sodas and juices, release sugar into the body quickly. These foods have been associated with cardiovascular disease, possibly because of protein cross-linking.

### Free Radicals Age You

Free radicals are a byproduct of normal cell function and when cells create energy, they also produce unstable oxygen molecules. These molecules are called free radicals and have a free electron. This electron makes the molecule highly unstable. The free radical bonds to other molecules in the body causing proteins and other essential molecules to not function as they should. Luckily, antioxidants can minimize free radical damage.

### Antioxidants - the Free Radical Sponge

Antioxidants are substances found in plants that counteract free radicals by acting as sponges. If plenty of antioxidants are available, it can minimize the damage caused by free radicals. The best antioxidants come from eating plants. There is some evidence that we can only get the full antioxidant benefits from eating real plants and other foods. Supplements do not appear to be as effective.

### How Free Radicals Cause Aging:

Many of the changes that occur as our bodies age are caused by free radicals. Damage to DNA, protein cross-linking and other changes has been attributed to free radicals. This damage is known to accumulate and causes us to experience aging. There is some evidence that has shown that increasing the amount of antioxidants in the diets of mice and other animals can slow the effects of aging. This theory does not fully explain all the changes that occur during aging. It is likely that free radicals are only one part in the aging equation.

## We Become Mutants

An important part of aging is determined by what happens to our genes after we inherit them. From the time of conception, our body's cells are continually reproducing. Each time a cell divides; there is a chance that some of the genes will be copied incorrectly. This is called a mutation and additionally, exposures to toxins, radiation or ultraviolet light can causes mutations in your body's genes. The body can correct or destroy most of the mutations, but not all of them. Eventually the mutated cells accumulate and copy themselves resulting in problems in the body's functioning related to aging.

## Not the Same as Genetic Aging Theory:

Genetic aging is only concerned with the genes in sperm and egg cells. Those are the genes that can be passed down from generation to generation. Somatic mutations are changed in the genes that occur after you have inherited them, but cannot be passed down to your children. The somatic mutation theory only explains a piece of the puzzle. Of course, there is evidence of gene mutations causing damage and even death, but it cannot be said that this is the most important factor in aging.

## Chapter 2 - Is Life Extension Possible?

The term life extension deals exclusively with a wide variety of approaches that share the goal of extending life. Many of these approaches are simply theories based on our understanding of why we age. Some, however, are more science fiction than science and some can even be classified as outright entertainment.

Currently, theories exist that we are capable of extending the human life span out to as many as 5,000 years by the end of the century using biogenetics. That, of course, on the surface is absurd. As stated above, living a healthy lifestyle and avoiding risks doesn't even guarantee adding years to your life. Here is a summary of some of the latest theories and approaches:

## Calorie Restriction

Much of the damage due to aging in the body is caused by the metabolic process of converting food into energy. If we can limit the amount of food by 30 to 50 percent, then we can limit the damage due to aging. Researchers have been able to almost double the life span of rats in the laboratory through a 30 to 50 percent calorie restricted diet. Studies have also been done successfully in primates that extend life somewhat and prevent many age-related illnesses. No studies have been completed in humans, though there are people who are attempting a calorie-restricted diet. Time will tell if they live longer than average.

## Nutritional Approaches

Supplying the body with more antioxidants and other nutritional elements will help to slow the process of aging. By giving the body more antioxidants, damage by free radicals is lessened. It is not clear whether these approaches slow the actual aging process, or merely reduce an individual's risk of illness. No studies have linked these nutritional approaches with an actual increase in life span though they are linked with a decrease in illness. Supplements have been shown not as effective as eating real food. The oldest advice is still the best advice: Eat Lots of Fruits and Vegetables.

## Hormone Replacement Therapy

As people age, their levels of hormones, especially human growth hormone, testosterone and DHEA, all decline. Hormone replacement therapy gives people doses of these hormones to counteract the effects and impact of aging. A person taking some hormone replacement therapy will feel better for a time. But the supplements are likely to slow down, not speed up, the body's own ability to make these important hormones. No evidence exists to link hormone replacement therapy with increased life span in humans.

## Body Part Replacement

The human body is like a house, over time, you can replace the roof, change the doors and ever redo the kitchen but the house itself survives. Adherents to this theory believe that through human cloning, stem cell research and other new technologies, we will be able to grow and replace body parts as they wear out. We can expect more body part replacement in the future, but this approach is unlikely to counteract aging itself. The wear and tear theory of aging that is behind the logic of body part replacement does not take into account the systemic changes that occur over time.

## Cryonics

If you can stop your life's clock from ticking in an ageless state of suspended animation, then you can wait for new technologies to come along to cure illnesses, replace your organs and keep you living. Cryonics adherents believe that by reducing body temperature in a complex process that prevents freezing but chills the body to extremely low temperatures, one can preserve cells and tissues indefinitely. Very little evidence exists to suggest that cryonics works. No mammal has ever been successful cryo-preserved and brought back to life. The standard practice with humans is to place a person in a cryogenic state immediately upon death, but before the degeneration of tissues and cells. This is done in the hopes that someday in the future, medicine will not only be able to revive a person from this state, but also be able to treat whatever caused death in the first place.

## Chapter 3 - Hydrogen Sulfide and Longevity - Life Extension and Hibernation

Can any chemical placed into your body cause a kind of cellular hibernation? That is what research at the Fred Hutchinson Cancer Research Center is trying to figure out. Researchers have used a chemical known as Hydrogen Sulfide (H2S) to put mice into a "reverse metabolic hibernation."

### Life Extension, Longevity and Hydrogen Sulfide

This study takes hydrogen sulfide and put it in nematodes (tiny worms). When the nematodes lived in an environment where the air contained a low concentration of hydrogen sulfide, the worms did not hibernate metabolically, but their life span and heat tolerance still increased. This was repeated 15 times for confirmation and 77% of the exposed worms lived an average of 9.6 days longer than the non-exposed "control worms."

Researchers ruled out some complex explanations involving insulin and other genetic pathways. They now believe that the hydrogen sulfide helps regulate the SIR-2.1 gene, a gene known to be important in longevity. When this gene is "overactive," it can increase the lifespan of other worms (c. elegans) by 20%.

While the nematode has enough similarities with humans to be a great research model, there really isn't any evidence that living in an environment with higher hydrogen sulfide levels will extend life in humans. Researchers are excited about this line of research as a way of potentially "buying time" for critically ill patients by slowing their metabolism while waiting for treatment to take effect.

But if you would like your nematodes to live 70% longer, you might consider this.

## Chapter 4 - Calorie Restriction and Life Extension & Calorie Restriction and Life Expectancy - Cut Calories, Live Longer?

### Calorie Restriction:

Calorie restriction is a strategy to increase life expectancy by reducing the total amount of calories consumed daily. Calorie restriction research has been around since the 1930s and recent studies have shown longevity benefits to rats and other animals from a low calorie diet. Calorie restriction is thought to prevent or improve numerous health conditions, especially ones related to cardiovascular disease and diabetes.

In calorie restriction, nutritional choices are very important. Calorie-poor, nutrient-dense foods such as vegetables are chosen over sugars, high carbohydrate items and other foods. Anyone using a calorie restriction diet should be well-educated on nutrition and have regular check-ups with their doctor.

On average, the typical American consumes between 2000 and 3000 calories per day. Someone practicing calorie restriction may consume between 1500 and 2000 daily calories.

The maximum lifespan of rats has been nearly doubled in some experiments by placing the rats on a nutritious, low calorie diet. Other animals have also been used to prove the benefits of calorie restriction including monkeys, mice, and spiders.

Not only do the animals on calorie restriction live longer, they remain more youthful, energetic and healthy.

In humans, calorie restriction has been shown to lower blood pressure, improve the function of heart, veins, and arteries, and lower blood insulin levels.

No one really knows if calorie restriction can increase the life expectancy in humans.

# Chapter 5 - Can Suspended Animation Extend Life? - Suspended Animation...

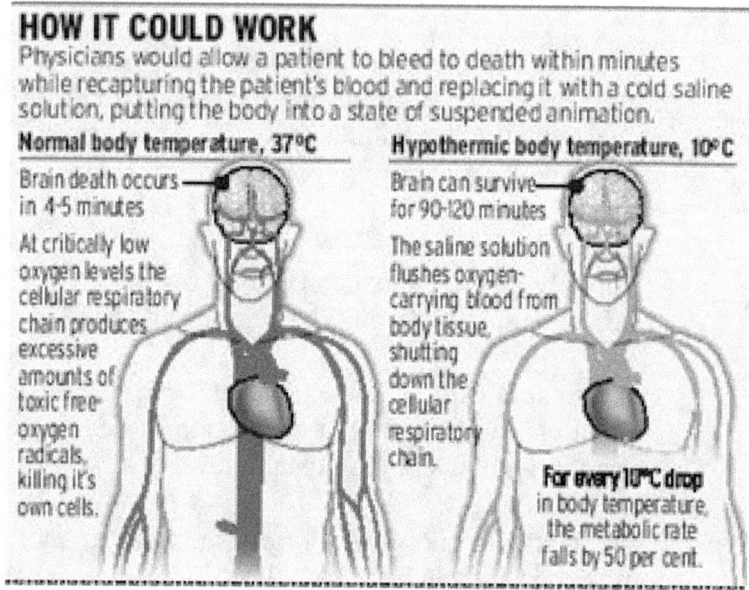

## HOW IT COULD WORK

Physicians would allow a patient to bleed to death within minutes while recapturing the patient's blood and replacing it with a cold saline solution, putting the body into a state of suspended animation.

**Normal body temperature, 37°C**

Brain death occurs in 4-5 minutes

At critically low oxygen levels the cellular respiratory chain produces excessive amounts of toxic free oxygen radicals, killing it's own cells.

**Hypothermic body temperature, 10°C**

Brain can survive for 90-120 minutes

The saline solution flushes oxygen-carrying blood from body tissue, shutting down the cellular respiratory chain.

For every 10°C drop in body temperature, the metabolic rate falls by 50 per cent.

Can Suspended Animation Extend Life? Suspended animation is the process of slowing metabolism and other activity associated with living through external means (such as applying cold) without causing death.

This idea has led to all sorts of science fiction applications of suspended animation; the most common example is putting the idea of putting astronauts in suspended animation during space flights of incredibly long duration. When people typically think of suspended animation and life extension, they often get confused between suspended animation and the idea of cryonics.

In cryonics, a person is literally frozen using liquid nitrogen. The person is, technically, dead. The cryonics proponents believe that, as technology develops, a frozen person could be reanimated, or brought back to life. Some (very rich people) have chosen to have their bodies frozen at the moment of death using cryonics with the idea that, decades or centuries from now, they could be reanimated and the cause of their death can be treated. I would say this is science fiction, expect that the freezing part has already happened; what hasn't happened is that whole reviving and treating part in the future.

Suspended animation, however, is an entirely different thing. Doctors are looking into the possibilities of placing a person in a state of suspended animation during certain surgical procedures to, in essence, buy time to fix things. Not only that, but there are other ways to achieve suspended animation than simply making a body cold (such as hydrogen sulphide gas in the correct dosage which suspends that need for oxygen in the body). There has been research in which animals were revived after being in a "technically dead" state for three hours. This line of research is funded by the National Institutes of Health and other scientific organizations.

If suspended animation can be developed for use in trauma and other situations, it would have the potential to increase the survival rate from these procedures, thereby extending life.

**Bottom Line**

Suspended animation has the potential to extend life in the next decade or so by giving surgeons additional tools to "buy time" to transport patients to the point of care and to allow for longer, more complex, surgical procedures.

## Chapter 6 - Is Aging in Our Genes? Aging and Genetics - Genes and Successful Aging, DNA, genes & chromosomes, why enzymes are important

Some families have a long history of aging well while others seem to have a history of age-related health problems. But is it because the families have "good" or "bad" aging genes? Or is it because families tend to have the same behaviors and habits in each generation?

Studying this in humans is really, really difficult. There are too many variables and it takes too long to get data about life expectancy. Worms, on the other hand, are great for this type of study -- specifically a tiny worm called a nematode (you may have dissected these in high school biology class).

Nematodes are an amazing research subject for aging and genetics studies because they don't live very long (you don't have to wait a long time for results) and their genome (genetic code) is mapped and not overwhelmingly big.

In aging research, two types of aging are studied: chronological age (the amount of time an organism has lived) and physiological age (how healthy you are). For example, a man can be age 70, but his body may be more like that of a 50-year-old (known as successful aging). Or, he may be 70 and his body functions more like a 90-year-old (poor aging). Trying to figure out the physiological age of people is a multi-million dollar business. Trying to figure out the physiological age of nematodes is simply research.

To test aging in worms, the researchers put the nematodes in dangerous situations that cause the worms to react. The scientists then measured their speed, dexterity, etc. Over time, a database was built that showed the average and extreme reactions of elderly nematodes.

Next, researchers took all the data and looked into the DNA and genetics of the nematodes. Looking at genetic information alone, they could predict, with 70% accuracy, the difference between the nematode's chronological age and physiological age.

## So Am I Doomed By My Genes?
Nematodes are pretty simple organisms and they all grew up in very controlled environments in the lab. The analogy for people would be to take people and keep

them all in the same house, feed them the same food and give them the same amount of activity over their entire lives. Some of them will age well and others will not and we could determine who had the best genes for that environment.

But we live in a world with lots of change and variation. Some people may have a gene for high cholesterol that leads to heart problems only if exposed to a poor diet (but if they were a strict vegetarian, this gene would not be a problem). So the key is to understand the genetic factors and adjust/optimize your lifestyle to minimize risk.

We aren't there yet, but expect more genetic health information to come out that impacts aging. Be prepared to make adjustments to your life to accommodate a bad gene here and there. And don't get too caught up in all this genetics and aging talk.

You and I both know what we need to do to be healthier: eat right, exercise, de-stress, have more fun and sleep better. These things we can change, our genetics we can't.

## Chapter 7 - New Scientific Breakthroughs – Mitochondrial and Aging

### Mitochondrial Electron Transport Chain

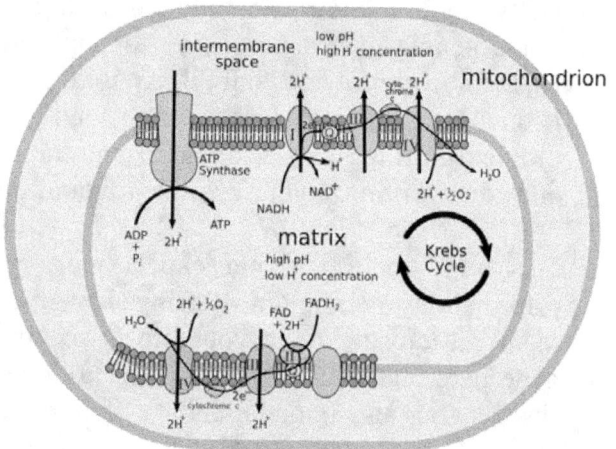

## IS THERE AN AGE LIMIT?

One hundred and twenty years, as far as we know, is the longest that anyone has ever lived. A man in Japan, Shirechiyo Izumi, reached the age of 120 years, 237 days in 1986, according to documents that most experts think are authentic. He died after developing pneumonia. Long lives always make us wonder: What is the secret? Does it lie in the genes? Is it where people live or the way they live -- something they do or do not do? Eat or do not eat? Most of the scientists who study aging, gerontologists, say the secret probably lies in all of the above -- heredity, environment, and lifestyle.

But gerontologists also ask other and more difficult questions. For example, if the 120-year-old had not finally succumbed to illness, could he have lived on and on? Or was he approaching some built-in, biological limit? Is there a maximum human life span beyond which we cannot live no matter how optimal our environment or favorable our genes? Whether or not there is such a limit, what happens as we age? What are the dynamics of this process and how do they make life spans short, average, or long? Once we understand these dynamics, could they be used to extend everyone's life span to 120 or even, as some scientists speculate, to much greater ages?

And finally for all of us, the most important question: How can insights into longevity be used to fight the diseases and disabilities associated with old age to make sure this period of life is healthy, active, and independent? In Search of the Secrets of Aging describes what we know so far about the answers to these questions and what we want to know. It gives an overview of research on aging and longevity, showing the major puzzle pieces already in place and, to the extent possible, the shapes of those that are missing

## The Genetic Connection
In laboratories around the country, scientists are isolating specific genes, cloning them, mapping them to chromosomes, and studying their products to learn what they do and how they influence aging and longevity. Humans seem to have a maximum life span of about 120 years, but for tortoises it's 150 and for dogs, about 20. What underlies these differences among species are

genes, the coded segments of DNA (deoxyribonucleic acid) strung like beads along the chromosomes of nearly every living cell. In humans, the nucleus of each cell holds 23 pairs of chromosomes, and together these chromosomes contain about 100,000 genes. The link between genes and life span is unquestioned. The simple observation that some species live longer than others -- humans longer than dogs, tortoises longer than mice -- is one convincing piece of evidence. Another comes from recent, dramatic laboratory studies in which researchers, through selective breeding or genetic engineering, have been able to raise animals with extended life spans. For example, fruit flies bred selectively have lived nearly twice as long as average.

**Longevity Genes**
By demonstrating that genes are linked to life span, the long-lived fruit flies have set the stage for more questions. What specific genes are involved? What activates them? How do they influence aging and longevity? In numerous laboratories, the search for answers is on. Some leads are coming from yeast cells in which researchers have found evidence of 14 genes that seem to be related to aging (see Tracking Down a Longevity Gene, page 10). Longevity-related genes have also been found in tiny worms called nematodes and in fruit flies. Like yeast, nematodes and fruit flies have short life spans and their genes, which are known and do not vary greatly, are relatively easy to study.

**In the Lab of the Long-Lived Fruit Flies**
A laboratory at the University of California, Irvine, is the home of thousands of Drosophila melanogaster or fruit

flies that routinely live for 70 or 80 days, nearly twice the average Drosophila life span. Here evolutionary biologist Michael Rose has bred the long-lived stocks by selecting and mating flies late in life. To begin the process of genetic selection, Rose first collected eggs laid by middle-aged fruit flies and let them hatch in isolation. The progeny were then transferred to a communal Plexiglas cage to eat, grow, and breed under conditions ideal for mating. Once they had reached advanced ages, the eggs laid by older females (and fertilized by older males) were again collected and removed to individual hatching vials. The cycle was repeated, but with succeeding generations, the day on which the eggs were collected was progressively postponed. After two years and 15 generations, the laboratory had stocks of Drosophila with longer life spans.

The next question is what genes and what gene products are involved? Since the first experiments, Rose has bred longer life spans into fruit flies by selecting for other characteristics, such as ability to resist starvation, so the flies' long life spans are not necessarily tied to their fertility late in life. One possibility is that the anti-oxidant enzyme, superoxide dismutase (SOD), is involved. In another laboratory at Irvine, the late Robert Tyler discovered that the longer-lived flies had a somewhat different form of the SOD gene, which was more active than its counterpart in the flies with average life spans. This finding has given a boost to the hypothesis that anti-oxidant enzymes like SOD are linked to aging or longevity.

Some of the genes found in yeast and fruit flies seem to promote longevity. But others may shorten life span. One such "death gene" has been isolated in nematodes by researchers at the University of Colorado in Boulder, who found that mutation of a certain gene more than doubles the nematode's normal 3-week life span. Thomas Johnson's laboratory in Boulder has also uncovered evidence that the mutant may extend life span by overproducing superoxide dismutase (SOD) and catalase, two anti-oxidant enzymes that have been linked to longevity in other studies. The genes isolated so far are only a few of what scientists think may be dozens, perhaps hundreds, of longevity- and aging-related genes. Tracking them down in organisms like nematodes and yeast is just the beginning. The next big question for many gerontologists is whether there are counterparts in people -- human homologs -- of the genes found in laboratory animals.

Other unanswered questions concern the roles played by these genes. What exactly do they do? On one level, all genes function by transcribing their "codes" -- actually DNA base sequences -- into another nucleic acid called messenger ribonucleic acid or mRNA. Messenger RNA is then translated into proteins. Transcription and translation together constitute the process known as gene expression. The proteins expressed by genes carry out a multitude of functions in each cell and tissue in the body, and some of these functions are related to aging. So when we ask what longevity- or aging-related genes do, we are actually asking what their protein products do at the cellular and tissue levels. Increasingly, gerontologists are also asking how alterations in the process of gene expression itself may affect aging. Some proteins, such as anti-oxidants, appear to prevent damage to cells, and others may repair damaged DNA or help cells respond to stress; more about these comes later. Other gene products are thought to control cell senescence, a process that could prove to be a key piece in the puzzle of aging and longevity.

**Cell Senescence**
Picture a cell: the threadlike pairs of chromosomes inhabit a nucleus that floats in a sea of cytoplasm along with other tiny organelles that do the cell's work, the whole surrounded by a membrane at the surface of which the cell sends and receives messages from other cells. Then picture the chromosomes, condensing into rod-like structures that divide in two, the nucleus disappearing, the chromosomes migrating to opposite sides of the cell where other nuclei are formed, and after that the entire cell following the chromosomes' lead, pulling apart and forming two identical daughter cells. This, the process of mitosis, or asexual cell division, takes place in nearly all of the 100 trillion or so cells that make up the human body. But it does not go on indefinitely. About the middle of this century, researchers learned that cells have finite life spans, at least when studied in test tubes -- in vitro.

A built-in limit on cell division may help explain the aging process. After a certain number of divisions, they enter a state of cell senescence, in which they do not divide or proliferate and DNA synthesis is blocked. For example, young human fibroblasts -- collagen-producing cells frequently used in this branch of aging research -- divide about 50 times and then stop. This phenomenon has become known as the Hayflick limit, after Leonard

Hayflick, who with Paul Moorhead first described it while at the Wistar Institute in Philadelphia. Intrigued by the possibility that the Hayflick limit might help explain some aspects of bodily aging, gerontologists have looked for and found links between senescence and human life spans. Fibroblasts taken from 75-year-olds, for example, have fewer divisions remaining than cells from a child. Moreover, the longer a species' life span, the higher its Hayflick limit; human fibroblasts have higher Hayflick limits than mice fibroblasts.

## Proliferative Genes

Searching for explanations of proliferation and senescence, scientists have found certain genes that appear to trigger cell proliferation. One example of such a proliferative gene is c-fos, which encodes a short-lived protein that is thought to regulate the expression of other genes important in cell division. But c-fos and others of its kind are countered by anti-proliferative genes, which seem to interfere with division. The first evidence of an anti-proliferative gene came from an eye tumor called retinoblastoma.

When one of the genes from retinoblastoma cells -- later called the RB gene -- became inactive, the cells went on dividing indefinitely and produced a tumor. But when the RB gene product was activated, the cells stopped dividing. This gene's product, in other words, appeared to suppress proliferation. Senescence is the norm in the world of cells. In some cases, however, a cell somehow escapes this control mechanism and goes on dividing, becoming, in the terms of cell biology, immortal. And because immortal cells eventually form tumors, this is one area in which aging research and cancer research intersect. Investigators theorize that a failure of anti-proliferative genes (also known as tumor suppressor genes) is the first step in a complex process that leads to development of a tumor. Senescence, according to this view, may have evolved because it protected against cancer.

Still a mystery is how these genes' products function to promote and suppress cell proliferation. There are indications that a multi layer control system is at work, involving probably a host of intricate mechanisms that interact to maintain a balance between the two kinds of genes. Many gerontologists are now involved in unraveling these intricacies, studying both the genes and their products to learn which ones influence senescence and how.

**Tracking Down a Longevity Gene**
Investigators are finding clues to aging and longevity in yeast, one-celled organisms that have some intriguing genetic similarities to human cells. In a laboratory at Louisiana State University Medical Center in New Orleans, Michal Jazwinski has found genes that seem to promote longevity in these rapidly dividing, easy-to-study organisms. Yeast normally has about 21 cell divisions or generations. Jazwinski observed that over the course of that "life span," certain genes in the yeast are more active or less active as the cells age; in the language of molecular biology, they are differentially expressed. So far, Jazwinski has found 14 such genes in yeast. Selecting one of these genes, Jazwinski tried two different experiments. First, he introduced the gene into

yeast cells in a form that allowed him to control its activity. When the gene was activated to a greater degree than normal, or over expressed, some of the yeast cells went on dividing for 27 or 28 generations; their period of activity was extended by 30 percent.

In his second experiment, Jazwinski mutated the gene. When he introduced this non-working version into a group of yeast cells, they had only about 12 divisions. The two experiments made it clear that the gene, now called LAG-1, influences the number of divisions in yeast or, according to some researchers' ways of thinking, its longevity. (LAG-1 is short for longevity assurance gene.) But how it works is still a mystery. One small clue lies in its sequence of DNA bases -- its genetic code -- which suggests that it produces a protein found in cell membranes. One next step is to study the function of that protein. Similar sequences have been found in human DNA, so a second investigative path is to clone the human gene and study its function. If there turns out to be a human LAG-1 counterpart, new insights into aging may be uncovered.

### Telomeres
In the meantime, scientists are finding more clues to senescence in the architecture of DNA. Every chromosome, they have discovered, has tails at the ends that get shorter as a cell divides. Named telomeres, the tails all have the same, short sequence of DNA bases repeated thousands of times. The repetitive structure stabilizes the chromosomes, forming a tight bond between the two strands of the DNA. Each time a cell divides, the telomeres shed a number of bases, so

telomere length gives some indication of how many divisions the cell has already undergone and how many remain before it becomes senescent.

This apparent counting mechanism, almost like an abacus keeping track of the cell's age, has led to speculation that telomeres do serve as molecular meters of cell division. But they may play a more active role, and telomere researchers are exploring the possibility that these chromosome ends regulate cellular life span in some way. The repeated DNA bases in telomeres form tight bonds that help stabilize chromosomes. About 50 bases are lost from each telomere every time a normal cell divides. Telomere research is another territory where cancer and aging research merge. In immortal cancer cells, telomeres act abnormally -- they stop shrinking with each cell division. In the search for clues to this phenomenon, researchers have zeroed in on an enzyme called telomerase. Normally absent in adult cells, telomerase seems to swing into action in advanced cancers, enabling the telomeres to replace lost sequences and divide indefinitely. This finding has led to speculation that if a drug could be developed to block telomerase activity, it might aid in cancer treatment.

Whether cell senescence is explained by abnormal gene products, telomere shortening, or other factors, the question of what senescence has to do with the aging of organism's remains and continues to be the focus of intense study. In the meantime, gerontologists are also studying proteins in the body that may play a role in aging and longevity. Genes hold the codes to these proteins, but what substances turn the genes on and off?

41

And once activated, how do their products interact with the products of other genes? What is their effect on cells and tissues? The biochemistry of aging holds some of the answers.

## Biochemistry and Aging

Proteins, in their myriad forms and functions, are the substances most responsible for the day-to-day functioning of living organisms. Some of these proteins seem to affect the way we age and how long we live. Treacherous oxygen molecules, protective enzymes, hormones that seem to turn back the clock, and proteins that may speed it up: The biochemistry of aging is a rich territory with an expanding frontier. Major areas of exploration include oxygen radicals and glucose cross linking of proteins, both of which damage cells; the substances that help prevent and repair damage; and the role of specific proteins, particularly heat shock proteins, hormones, and growth factors.

## Oxygen Radicals

Demolishing proteins and damaging nucleic acids, oxygen radicals are thought to be the villains in the day-to-day life of cells. The free radical theory of aging, first proposed by Denham Harman at the University of Nebraska, holds that damage caused by oxygen radicals is responsible for many of the bodily changes that come with aging.

Free radicals have been implicated not only in aging but also in degenerative disorders, including cancer, atherosclerosis, cataracts, and neurodegeneration. They damage cells and may cause tissues and organs to age. A free radical is a molecule with an unpaired, highly reactive electron. An oxygen-free radical is a byproduct of normal metabolism, produced as cells turn food and oxygen into energy.

In need of a mate for its lone electron, the free radical takes an electron from another molecule, which in turn becomes unstable and combines readily with other molecules. A chain reaction can ensue, resulting in a series of compounds, some of which are harmful. They damage proteins, membranes, and nucleic acids, particularly DNA, including the DNA in mitochondria, the organelles within the cell that produce energy. But free radicals do not go unchecked. Mounted against them is a multi layer defense system manned by anti-oxidants that react with and disarm these damaging molecules. Anti-oxidants include nutrients -- the familiar vitamins C and E and beta carotene -- as well as enzymes, such as superoxide dismutase (SOD), catalase, and glutathione peroxidase. They prevent most, but not all, oxidative damage. Little by little the damage mounts and contributes, so the theory goes, to deteriorating tissues and organs.

Support for the free radical theory comes from studies of anti-oxidants, particularly SOD. SOD converts oxygen radicals into the also harmful hydrogen peroxide, which is then degraded by another enzyme, catalase, to oxygen and water.

Anti-Oxidants and Aging Gerbils

A boost for the hypothesis that high levels of anti-oxidants can slow the aging process comes from a study of N-tert-butyl-alpha-phenylnitrone or PBN in gerbils.

Although it does not occur naturally in the body, PBN works in much the same way as beta-carotene and other anti-oxidants by binding and neutralizing free radicals.

Older gerbils had been shown to have increased levels of oxidized protein in their brains by two researchers, Robert A. Floyd at the Oklahoma Medical Research Foundation and John M. Carney at the University of Kentucky. Curious about the effects of anti-oxidants in older animals, Floyd and Carney designed an experiment to learn whether PBN could lower oxidized protein levels in gerbils' brains. Over a period of 14 days they gave PBN to two groups of gerbils, one made up of young adults, the other of older adults.

As the older gerbils were treated with PBN, their levels of oxidized protein decreased until they were nearly comparable to levels found in the younger animals. After treatment ended, oxidized protein gradually returned to pretreatment levels. PBN had no effect on the young gerbils.

While it is only one study and more are needed, this investigation supports the idea that maintaining anti-oxidant defense levels may be critical during aging. It also suggests that an intervention such as PBN may someday provide the means.

At the National Institute on Aging (NIA), Richard Cutler has found that SOD levels are directly related to life span in 20 different species; longer-lived animals have higher levels of SOD, suggesting that the ability to fight free radicals has something to do with longer life spans.

Levels of other anti-oxidants -- vitamin E and beta-carotene, for example -- have also been correlated with life span.

Other studies have shown that inserting extra copies of the SOD gene into fruit flies extends their average life span. In three different laboratories, researchers have reported that transgenic fruit flies, carrying extra copies of the gene for SOD, live 5 to 10 percent longer than average.

Other experimental evidence lends support to the free radical hypothesis. For example, higher levels of SOD and catalase have been found in long-lived nematodes. And in another important study, giving gerbils a synthetic anti-oxidant has reduced high levels of oxidized protein, a sign of aging, in their brains.

The discovery of anti-oxidants raised hopes that people could retard aging simply by adding them to the diet. Unfortunately taking SOD tablets has no effect on cellular aging; the enzyme is simply broken down in the body during digestion.

And when anti-oxidant vitamins are added to cells, they compensate by halting production of their own anti-oxidants, leaving free radical levels unchanged.

Researchers have not abandoned all hope for dietary anti-oxidants, however. Current studies, for example, are exploring the possibility that vitamin C can reduce heart disease by blocking oxidation of low-density lipoproteins. Oxidation of these cholesterol-carrying proteins is thought to be a key element in hardening of the arteries. In addition, there is evidence that vitamin E in the diet may be linked to heart attacks, with low vitamin E intake appearing to increase the risk.

## Glucose Cross linking
Another suspect in cellular deterioration is blood sugar or glucose. In a process called non-enzymatic glycosylation or glycation, glucose molecules attach themselves to proteins, setting in motion a chain of chemical reactions that ends in the proteins binding together or cross linking, thus altering their biological and structural roles. The process is slow but increases with time.

Cross links, which have been termed advanced glycosylation end products (AGEs), seem to toughen tissues and may cause some of the deterioration associated with aging. AGEs have been linked to stiffening connective tissue (collagen), hardened arteries, clouded eyes, loss of nerve function, and less efficient kidneys.

These are deficiencies that often accompany aging. They also appear at younger ages in people with diabetes, who have high glucose levels. Diabetes, in fact, is sometimes considered an accelerated model of aging. Not only do its complications mimic the physiologic changes that can accompany old age, but its victims have shorter-than-average life expectancies. As a result, much research on cross linking has focused on its relationship to diabetes as well as aging.

One happy finding is that the body has its own defense system against cross linking. Just as it has anti-oxidants to fight free-radical damage, it has other guardians, immune system cells called macrophages that combat glycation. Macrophages with special receptors for AGEs seek them out, engulf them, break them down, and eject them into the blood stream where they are filtered out by the kidneys and eliminated in urine.

Glucose, the fundamental source of energy, reacts with and cross links essential molecules. The only apparent drawback to this defense system is that it is not complete and levels of AGEs increase steadily with age. One reason is that kidney function tends to decline with advancing age. Another is that macrophages, like certain other components of the immune system, become less active. Why is not known, but immunologists are beginning to learn more about how the immune system affects and is affected by aging. And in the meantime, diabetes researchers are investigating drugs that could supplement the body's natural defenses by blocking AGE formation.

Cross linking interests gerontologists for several reasons. It is associated with disorders that are common among older people, such as diabetes; it progresses with age; and AGEs are potential targets for anti-aging drugs. In addition, cross linking may play a role in damage to DNA, which has become another important focus for research on aging.

**DNA Repair**
In the normal wear and tear of cellular life, DNA undergoes continual damage. Attacked by oxygen

radicals, ultraviolet light, and other toxic agents, it suffers damage in the form of deletions, or destroyed sections, and mutations, or changes in the sequence of DNA bases that make up the genetic code.

Biologists theorize that this DNA damage, which gradually accumulates, leads to malfunctioning genes, proteins, cells, and, as the years go by, deteriorating tissues and organs. Not surprisingly, numerous enzyme systems in the cell have evolved to detect and repair damaged DNA. The repair process interests gerontologists. It is known that an animal's ability to repair certain types of DNA damage is directly related to the life span of its species. Humans repair DNA, for example, more quickly and efficiently than mice or other animals with shorter life spans. This suggests that DNA damage and repair are in some way part of the aging puzzle.

In addition, researchers have found defects in DNA repair in people with a genetic or familial susceptibility to cancer. If DNA repair processes decline with age while damage accumulates, as scientists hypothesize, it could help explain why cancer is so much more common among older people.

Gerontologists who study DNA damage and repair have begun to uncover numerous complexities. Even within a single organism, repair rates can vary among cells, with the most efficient repair going on in terms (sperm and egg) cell. Moreover, certain genes are repaired more quickly than others, including those that regulate cell proliferation.

## Frontiers

Gerontology is headed toward a deeper understanding of aging in the search for ways to make it a healthier process.

New territory, unexplored or only sketchily mapped, lies ahead. As gerontologists isolate and characterize more and more longevity- and aging-related genes in laboratory animals, insights into genes and gene products important in human aging will emerge. Comparable human genes will be identified and mapped to chromosomes.

This information will be useful in designing both genetic and non-genetic interventions to slow or even reverse some aging-related changes. Already, for example, a study by Helen Blau of Stanford University has shown that muscle cells can be genetically modified and injected into muscle where they will produce and secrete human growth hormone. Non-genetic strategies will include the development of interventions to reduce damage to cellular components, such as proteins, nucleic acids, and lipids.

Normal aging will be more closely defined. For instance, at NIA's Gerontology Research Center, the behavior of the cells that line blood vessels during aging is now providing clues to the stiffening of blood vessels that occurs with age as well as insights into vascular disease. As key biomarkers of aging are identified, researchers will be able to use them to test interventions to slow aging. Studies will begin to delve more deeply into differences in aging between the sexes and among ethnic groups.

In short, gerontologists will be charting the paths and intersections of genetic, biochemical, and physiologic aging. What they find will reveal some of the secrets of aging. It may lead to extended life spans. It will very certainly contribute to better health, less disability, and more independence in the second fifty years of life.

## Chapter 8 - Aging Glossary

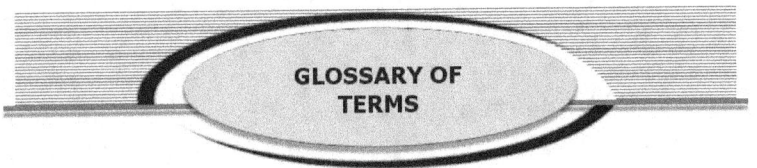

**Anti-oxidants** - Compounds that neutralize oxygen radicals. Some are enzymes like SOD while others are nutrients such as vitamin C, vitamin E, and beta-carotene. High levels of anti-oxidants have been associated with longer life spans.

**Anti-proliferative genes** - Genes that inhibit cell division or proliferation; also known as tumor suppressor genes.

**Average life span** - The average number of years that members of a population live.

**Biomarkers** - Biological changes that characterize the aging process; because biomarkers are considered a better measure of aging than chronological time, studies are underway to identify biomarkers in cells, tissues, and organs.

**Caloric restriction** - An experimental approach to studying longevity in which life spans of laboratory animals have been extended by reducing calories while the necessary level of nutrients is maintained.

**Cell senescence** - The stage at which a cell has stopped dividing permanently.

**Chromosomes** - Structures in the cell's nucleus, made up of protein and DNA that contain the genes.

**DNA (deoxyribonucleic acid)** - A large molecule that carries the genetic information necessary for all cellular functions, including the building of proteins; damage to DNA and the rate at which this damage is repaired may help determine the rate of aging.

**Free radicals** - Molecules with unpaired electrons that react readily with other molecules; oxygen-free radicals, produced during metabolism, damage cells and may be responsible for aging in tissues and organs.

**Gene** - A segment of DNA that contains the "code" for a specific protein or other product.

**Gene expression** - The process by which genes are transcribed and translated into proteins. Age-related changes in gene expression may account for some of the phenomena of aging.

**Glycation** - The process by which glucose links with proteins and causes them to bind together, thus stiffening tissues and leading to the complications of diabetes and perhaps some of the physiologic problems associated with aging.

**Hayflick limit** - The finite number of divisions of which at cell is capable.

**Interleukins** - Substances secreted by lymphocytes; their levels vary with age.

**Lymphocytes** - Small white blood cells that are important to the immune system. A decline in lymphocyte function with advancing age is being studied for insights into aging and disease.

**Maximum life span** - The greatest age reached by any member of a given species.

**Mitochondria** - Cell organelles that metabolize sugars into energy. Mitochondria also contain DNA, which is damaged by the high level of free radicals produced in the mitochondria.

**Proliferative genes** - Genes that promote cell division or proliferation; also known as oncogenes.

**Photo-aging** - The process initiated by sunlight through which the skin becomes drier and loses elasticity. Photo-aging is being studied for clues to aging because it has the same effect as normal aging on certain skin cells.

**Proteins** - Molecules make up of amino acids arranged in a specific order determined by the genetic code. Proteins are essential for all life processes. Certain ones, such as the enzymes that protect against free radicals and the lymphokines produced in the immune system, are being studied extensively by gerontologists.

## I Have a Special Gift for My Readers

I appreciate my readers for without them I am just another author attempting to make a difference. If my book has made a favorable impression please leave me an honest review.   Thank you in advance for you participation.

My readers and I have in common a passion for the written word as well as the desire to learn and grow from books.

My special offer to you is a massive ebook library that I have compiled over the years. It contains hundreds of fiction and non-fiction ebooks in Adobe Acrobat PDF format as well as the Greek classics and old literary classics too.

In fact, this library is so massive to completely download the entire library will require over 5 GBs open on your desktop.

Use the link below and scan all of the ebooks in the library. You can select the ebooks you want individually or download the entire library.

The link below does not expire after a given time period so you are free to return for more books rather than clog your desktop. And feel free to give the link to your friends who enjoy reading too.

I thank you for reading my book and hope if you are pleased that you will leave me an honest review so that I can improve my work and or write books that appeal to your interests.

Okay, here is the link…

http://tinyurl.com/special-readers-promo

PS: If you wish to reach me personally for any reason you may simply write to mailto:support@epubwealth.com.

I answer all of my emails so rest assured I will respond.

## Meet the Author

Dr. Noah Pranksky is a research behavioral scientist for Applied Mind Sciences. His research involves many aspects of the human mind including relationships, energy psychology, and various protocols and modalities relating to treatment and cure of various mental maladies.

He and his wife Marianne reside in Portland, Oregon.

**Visit some of his websites**
http://www.AddMeInNow.com
http://www.AppliedMindSciences.com
http://www.AppliedWebInfo.com
http://www.BookbuilderPLUS.com
http://www.BookJumping.com
http://www.EmailNations.com
http://www.EmbarrassingProblemsFix.com
http://www.ePubWealth.com
http://www.ForensicsNation.com

http://www.ForensicsNationStore.com
http://www.FreebiesNation.com
http://www.HealthFitnessWellnessNation.com
http://www.Neternatives.com
http://www.PrivacyNations.com
http://www.RetireWithoutMoney.org
http://www.SurvivalNations.com
http://www.TheBentonKitchen.com
http://www.Theolegions.org
http://www.VideoBookbuilder.com

www.ingramcontent.com/pod-product-compliance
Lightning Source LLC
Chambersburg PA
CBHW070351300526
45791CB00025B/2059